THE PLANO PLAN

Reformulating And Revitalizing Social Security

Robert L. Brielmaier

authorHOUSE®

AuthorHouse™
1663 Liberty Drive, Suite 200
Bloomington, IN 47403
www.authorhouse.com
Phone: 1-800-839-8640

First published by AuthorHouse 6/29/2007

ISBN: 978-1-4259-9384-9 (sc)

Library of Congress Control Number: 2007900819

Printed in the United States of America
Bloomington, Indiana

This book is printed on acid-free paper.

TABLE OF CONTENTS

An Introduction To The Problem

Two figures are haunting (or should be haunting) every person living in America in the first part of the 21st Century.

The first figure is Nine Trillion. Written as a number, the figure nine is followed by twelve zeroes: a terrifying 9,000,000,000,000. This is the present, Congressionally approved limit on the National Debt of the United States, or approximately $30,000 per American citizen. Alone this would be a major cause for concern, but when combined with a second figure, it becomes alarming.

The second figure is 77 million (77 followed by six zeroes) – the total of "Baby Boomers" who are presently collecting or soon will be collecting Social Security and Medicare benefits. This group of retirees (or soon to be retirees) forms about ¼ of the total population of the United States.

As originally envisioned in 1935, the Social Security Program was to be a pay-as-you-go system, with a 1% tax on an employee's paycheck (matched by an equal amount from his employer) financing monthly retirement benefits to a retiree when he reached age 65 and providing vital coverage for the worker's survivors, the permanently disabled, the unemployed, and those qualifying for public assistance. Over the years, "improvements" incorporated greater numbers of workers, increased the benefits granted, reduced the qualifications for public assistance, and lowered the minimum age for retirement.

The combined effect of these improvements and the increasing life span of the American worker has created a situation where within 15 years expenditures will exceed income by so great an amount that pay-as-you-go will no longer be sustainable. Meeting the increased expense by raising the basic Social Security payroll tax (over its present 6.2%) would require so high a rate that it cannot be considered as a possible option. But, if nothing is done by that point, America will either have to renounce completely the promises made to its senior citizens 70 years ago, cut back their benefits greatly (perhaps triggering a major recession and certainly imposing severe hardships on many seniors), or let the National Debt climb to an incredibly high (and an ultimately unsustainable) level.

Confronted with these altenatives, many concluded the United States was facing an imminent "Social Security Crisis" and demanded Congress prepare for this catastrophe by immediately implementing drastic measures to eliminate perceived fraud and abuse, raise either the Social Security or general tax rate (or perhaps both), slash other social programs, or severely cut the defense budget. While it is true that the Social Security Program as presently set up does require major alterations, there is not yet a "crisis". Happily, if instituted properly and promptly, the overhaul need not raise the taxes of most citizens, impair the benefits of present Social Security or other social program recipients, threaten the health of the national economy, nor severely impact the employees and employers supporting present retirees. Instead, by taking steps to once again make Social Security self-sustaining, a thoughtful reformulation of the program can free up additional funds for balancing the budget and eventually reducing the National Debt.

Generally, Congressmen and Senators wisely decide to make as minor and as few changes as necessary to handle a "looming crisis". While this is usually the wisest course to handle such situations, when the minor changes leave underlying problems unresolved, the "crisis" soon reappears, seemingly more threatening and insoluble than before. A far better way to handle recurring crises is to search out the major weaknesses causing the problem and eliminate them completely.

Rather than adding yet another patchwork amendment (to the 22 piecemeal amendments already made), Congress must think anew, reviewing the assumptions of 1935 and revising those assumptions in view of the present social and economic situation, rather than scuttling the program entirely, pig-headedly resisting any changes, or stupidly blathering devotion to Social Security and "sustainability" while being unwilling to make the reformulations needed to adjust to the realities of the 21st Century.

NO PROPOSAL PRESENTLY OFFERED CAN SAVE SOCIAL SECURITY FROM INSOLVENCY. IF THE PRESIDENT AND MEMBERS OF CONGRESS REMAIN UNWILLING TO ELIMINATE THE FALLACIES LONG PRESENTED ABOUT SOCIAL SECURITY AND CONTINUE TO INSIST UPON RETAINING ASSUMPTIONS THAT CHANGES IN THE ECONOMY AND SOCIETY HAVE PROVEN

FALSE, SOCIAL SECURITY'S BANKRUPTCY IS UNAVOIDABLE.

This, then, is where any suggestions for truly effective reform must begin. Unless the fallacies and assumptions since proven incorrect are addressed forthrightly before the debate about the details begins, any substantial change will be doomed by being labeled "too radical" or by arguments like "that's not the way the program was set up". The fact that 22 amendments have not permanently resolved Social Security's problems and crises are coming closer and closer together is perhaps the best proof that looking at changes that at one time seemed radical or re-examining the original assumptions may offer clues to the best solutions after all. The first section of this book will address those fallacies and incorrect assumptions.

The next step toward reformulating Social Security is to establish some basic guidelines that most reasonable people would find acceptable when implementing necessary reforms. The list need not be long, minutely detailed, or inclusive of what every person wants, but deciding beforehand what a rational person would consider just and what the final reformulation should include must guide discussion about what ought be included and what left untouched. The second section of this book will suggest five basic guidelines or principles that should direct the reform of the present Social Security program.

The final step in achieving change is to craft specific proposals. Each proposal should state the rationale for the change and how well it satisfies the agreed-upon guidelines. No guideline should be violated and the final overall package should show that all the guidelines have been incorporated into the final product. Surprisingly, when all of these principles are kept in mind, the alterations needed for the long-term welfare of Social Security become obvious and relatively easy to implement. The final five sections will offer specific proposals for change, each of which will satisfy all of the guidelines presented.

The chief danger that must be avoided in the discussion is pitting the interests of one group against those of another, or seeking an advantage for one party or its members over another by using "made for the voters" soundbites. The American voters want and deserve clear thinking followed by decisive action from their elected representatives. Actions win more votes than speeches. Political grandstanders and parties should bear in mind the penalties inflicted by voters on those unwilling to act and the rewards bestowed on those willing to take a stand.

The Republican President and Congress were repudiated in the 1932 elections because of their failure to act decisively to halt a deepening depression. As the humorist Will Rogers observed, the people wanted their elected officials to do something – anything. If President Roosevelt suggested burning down the Capitol (Rogers observed) people would applaud – at least the government was doing something. The New Deal had scant success in bringing about an economic recovery between 1933 and 1936, yet the Democratic Party increased its Congressional membership in 1934 and even more substantially in 1936, while Roosevelt swept all but Maine and Vermont in his 1936 reelection campaign. The economic problems had not been solved, but to most people that was not the most important thing: the Democratic Party was enacting specific programs to try to solve the problems facing the nation.

More recently, House Minority Leader Newt Gingrich convinced all his party's challengers to incumbents in the House of Representatives to sign a pledge to act on ten specific pieces of legislation if the voters elected a Republican majority. Though scoffed at initially, it was later cited to explain the upset giving the Republicans control of both the House and Senate in 1994 for the first time in 40 years. The Party had promised to "do something" specific, and the voters agreed to let them try.

The Social Security funding problem is not just going to go away or become less severe if we wait. The much touted Social Security Reserve built up since the last major "Permanent" Social Security reform (in 1980) is a myth ! With a virtual swarm of "Baby Boomers" reaching retirement in two years (1946 + 62 = 2008), there is precious little time to "DO SOMETHING" and every reason to act now without panic and get it done right.

This book will not employ a great amount of figures and statistics in explaining and defending these suggested proposals for reform. That is a task best left to accountants and mathematicians (often employing unstated, vague, or even foolish assumptions). Nor will it address the significant injustices in the program, such as the economic penalties for women who temporarily leave the paid workforce to care for children or their aging, bedridden parents, nor the long term harms (again primarily affecting women) of divorce and remarriage. These are problems best corrected by those more knowledgeable about these specific problems than I. Such just reforms ought to be included in any comprehensive reformulation.

I am neither an accountant, nor a mathematician, nor some sort of financial wizard. What I seek to do, and what I ask the reader to do, is to employ common sense about the future financing of Social Security retirement benefits. Correcting the injustices which have arisen due to the major societal changes since the original plan was set up (though necessary) need not significantly impact this funding plan. Since most of the suggestions are so simple and obvious to a person using common sense, nothing more is required from the reader.

Therefore with the simple request that he employ common sense and with no other matters to settle with the reader, I will begin.

Comments both favorable and unfavorable are always welcome:

Robert L. Brielmaier, 2305 Fountain Head Drive, Plano, Texas 75023   Phone (972) 596-5194
or   e-mail: robert_l_brielmaier@netzero.net

Misperceptions
and
Incorrect Assumptions

Before any serious discussion for reforming Social Security can begin, two serious misperceptions about Social Security must be dispelled, along with several assumptions made in 1935 which subsequently proved to be incorrect. Since these misperceptions and incorrect assumptions formed the foundation for the entire Social Security program and now inhibit major necessary changes, they must be eliminated before any real reformulation can be enacted.

Social Security has been portrayed from its inception as a combination insurance program for workers and their families and as a pay-as-you go account that can be redeemed at retirement (presently at or after age 62). This portrayal is false.

Social Security is not primarily an insurance policy for workers providing short term financial relief to a person who becomes unemployed through no fault of his own (such as by a corporation's downsizing, the obsolescence of his craft, or an economic recession) or a guarantee of life long payments for a permanently disabling injury sustained on the job. Nor is it a late-in-life insurance policy paying most of a person's medical and hospital expenses (and at least a portion of extraordinarily high prescription drug costs) after the person reaches age 65. Nor is it a sort of involuntary savings plan whereby a deduction taken from an employee's earnings (along with an equal amount added by his employer) is deposited in his personal "retirement account" from which he will receive benefits (with interest) when he retires or from which his dependents will receive payments if he dies before that. While Social Security does incorporate all of these features, the deductions made from all workers' paychecks are in essence a TAX.

Neither the worker nor his employer has the option of non-participation in the Social Security program, nor can either be exempted from the payments it demands. Over the years those subject to the Social Security tax has expanded. Today, over 90% of all workers make weekly Social Security payments. Whenever a government requires a person to pay a sum of money or a fee, regardless of the label it might choose to apply, that payment is a tax.

Abraham Lincoln once posed this question: "Suppose we called the tail of a dog a leg. How many legs does the ordinary dog have ?" The answer, of course, is four. Calling the tail a leg doesn't make it a leg. In the same way, my calling Social Security's weekly exaction a pay check guarantee, a health insurance policy for my later life, or a "contribution" to a special government pay-as-you-go retirement program doesn't make it anything other than a TAX .

Since the amount a person pays is directly related to the amount of money he earns, the Social Security tax is basically just another form of income tax. As the law is presently written, it is also indisputably the most regressive income tax levied in the United States.

Although more will be said later in the book about its regressive features, the important thing to remember is that the Social Security deduction from a worker's paycheck is just another form of taxation.

The second common misperception about Social Security is that this taxation is somehow "special" and that the money has been safely set aside in a "lock box" to pay future retirement benefits. As one of my friends used to say, "It just ain't so!"

Like the revenue raised from all taxes, the money collected is immediately spent to meet the general expenses of the government: defense, education, homeland security, highways … and the payment of Social Security retirement benefits, Medicare, and the new prescription drug benefit. The highly touted "Social Security Trust Fund Bonds", supposedly representing the extra money collected in excessive of payments made over the past few years (along with interest) and insuring future benefits, is nothing more than an accountant's fiction.

"Bonds" are financial instruments that can be bought, sold, or traded between two individuals or entities which impose an obligation on the bond issuer to make payments at stated intervals (interest) and to pay the full face value at some point in the future. But these "Social Security Trust Fund Bonds" cannot be acquired by anyone except the federal government, cannot be sold or traded to anyone, and can be cancelled by Congress at any time. No one (not even a government) can sell its bonds to itself nor feel free to cancel its obligations at any time at will ! These "bonds" are valueless sheets of paper (or perhaps, more kindly stated, a sort of receipt for money already spent).

Thus, the Social Security deduction is nothing more than another source of revenue, and payments to beneficiaries nothing more than another expenditure paid from general revenues of all sorts (including, in part, a worker's weekly payments to Social Security) with the amount to be paid at the total discretion of Congress. To state that future payments will be drawn from some "lock box" as Congress "redeems" those bonds ("its I.O.U.'s to future generations") is childish, cartoon-like thinking. Congress annually appropriates money for paying retirement benefits. Whether the payments are listed directly as an expenditure for the general welfare or indirectly as "the redemption of bonds" in the Social Security Trust Fund with the payments sent to retirees is as irrelevant as whether you pay your bills with money taken from your pocket or use your credit card.

But these two fallacies are not the only ideas that must be eliminated to allow for true Social Security reform. Rather than merely adding yet another patchwork amendment (to the 22 already made), Congress must think anew by reviewing the assumptions of 1935 and revise those assumptions to conform to modern reality. Congress can offer no rational plan to save Social Security from insolvency if it continues to insist upon acting under the assumptions of 1935 even after changes in the society and economy have shown them to be incorrect.

What then are the assumptions of 1935 that have subsequently been proven false ?

First false assumption: In a modern, highly industrialized country, like the United States, there will always be far more workers than retirees, sustaining a pay-as-you-go system.

In 1935 this was certainly true and seemed likely to continue forever, since there were 40 workers for every retiree. However, the ratio of workers to retirees has fallen ever since. By 1950, the ratio had shrunken to 16 to 1, and by the 1960's the ratio was 8 workers to support each retiree. Today the ratio is down to 3 to 1, with projections showing a slippage to 2 to 1 when the Baby-Boomers move into retirement (which begins in 2008). Obviously, two workers, unless excessively overpaid or exorbitantly taxed, cannot adequately support yet another person (the retiree). Indeed, for some companies in older industries, such as automobile manufacturing, the ratio has already reached absolute parity with the number of retirees equaling the number of workers supporting them.

Second false assumption: Life expectancy would remain near or just slightly above the set retirement age of 65. In 1935, the average life expectancy was 62. Although that had been increasing at a slow, steady rate, it was assumed few workers would actually live long enough to get their retirement benefits, and those who did reach retirement at 65 would receive payments for only a short time.

Now the overall average life expectancy has increased to 78+ years, and today's typical 60 year old can reasonably expect to reach 85. Two-thirds of the people who ever lived to 65 are alive today. Worse still for Social Security, life expectancy is likely to increase even more with the rise as quick as in previous years.

Third false assumption: An employee will work for one company his entire working career and will receive a generous, well-deserved pension, with clearly defined benefits, for the rest of his life.

Today many workers change not only companies but even occupations several times in their careers, and companies have proven themselves less concerned with the welfare of their former employees than in the past. In 1980, the percentage of workers receiving defined benefits from their employers after retirement (which, in addition to monthly pension payments, often include medical, dental, and vision insurance and some type of cost of living increases figured on an annual basis) was 83%; in the past 25 years, that percentage has plummeted to 21%. Today, 58% of assets for retirement are in "defined contribution" or in "self-directed accounts" (like 401k plans or IRA's, which pay back the amount put in plus interest), with only 42% of the assets dedicated to defined benefit plans. More disgracefully, a number of well known, national corporations forced long-term employees to switch from defined benefits to self-directed plans, denied any retirement benefits to new employees, or reneged on retirement promises entirely by seeking "bankruptcy relief protection".

Fourth false assumption: An employee could save money during his working years which, along with interest from his savings, a pension, and with Social Security as a supplement, would allow an adequate income following his retirement.

Today, 20% of workers expect earnings from a job to be a major source of income following their "retirement", and a recent poll by the AARP (an advocacy group for older Americans) found 31% of workers aged 40 or older had not yet saved any money for their retirement years. Twenty-eight percent of retirees admitted to not saving any money for retirement before leaving the work force. Fewer workers have personal savings accounts than in the past, and those who do receive such a meager rate of interest that they may as well bury their money in a tin can in their back yard. For many, without a pension and without any savings, Social Security has become the sole source of income during their "golden years".

Fifth false assumption: Although some employees earn substantially more than others, the difference will remain about the same or even decrease over the years. Since those better paid executives were already taxed more heavily than others, they should be exempt from paying an additional Social Security tax. In 1935, the Roosevelt Administration had gained passage of a graduated income tax, which was labeled as a "soak the rich" plan. To appease the Republican Party and the rich, the decision was made to impose a cap on how much of a worker's wages would be taxed.

However, the opposite of what was expected occurred. In many companies the gap between the best paid and the lowest paid employees has grown dramatically. Today, with the compensation committees of the Boards of Directors focusing on creating a total pay package for top executives of the company around the median of a comparative group of companies in the same industry, the pay given CEO's and other top company executives has spiraled upward rapidly, as the lowest paying companies boosted salaries and bonuses to exceed the median. Since the median is the midpoint with half of the salaries above and half the salaries below that figure, every increase to exceed the median raised that midpoint higher. Compounded by "performance objectives", often rewarding top executives with ten to twenty times their salaries, the gap between the top executives and the factory worker has widened. NEWSWEEK recently estimated that CEO's are now making 431 times more than the average worker (the biggest gap ever in the United States) and their pay had risen by over 500% since 1980. Even the miserly salaries given professional athletes have been replaced by multi-year contracts providing salaries in excess of $10 million annually. Shockingly, these astronomical "compensation packages" are scarcely touched by Social Security taxation.

Sixth false assumption: A medical benefit could safely be added to Social Security without substantially straining the entire retirement system, with the additional cost covered by a 1.45% increase in Social Security taxes. This addition was intended to allow access to adequate health care for those retired workers whose former employers did not include a medical insurance provision in their defined benefits retirement package.

Instead, the Medicare program has run a deficit from the start, with Congress annually using other general revenue funds to make up the difference. In 2005 alone, an additional 12% of the nation's largest companies terminated all health benefits for future retirees, while most others imposed higher co-pays or reduced or eliminated medical benefits as soon as their former workers were eligible for Medicare (at 65). Contending Medicare provided enough coverage, they shifted this expense from being their responsibility to the federal government. (It is interesting to note that the 1.45% increase did not impose any cap on earnings, which is characteristic of the rest of the Social Security taxation. Every employee's entire "compensation" is subject to this tax with his employer adding an equal amount.)

That many assumptions made 70 years ago (or in 1964 with regard to Medicare) have proven to be incorrect is obvious, and those erroneous assumptions now severely threaten the fundamental long-term solvency of Social Security. Congress would display a serious lack of common sense and courage if it did nothing more than simply amend Social Security for a 23rd time while leaving unexamined the misperceptions and erroneous assumptions which undermine the entire financial underpinnings of Social Security. Once the blinders of incorrect assumptions are removed, the reformulations necessary to create a comprehensive and financially sound program become obvious.

However, before rushing ahead, it is necessary to set some simple and fair guidelines for change, lest the reformed Social Security replaces misperceptions and faulty assumptions with unwise or unjust programs. Five suggested basic guidelines, which should be able to gain the support of all concerned with a rational Social Security program, are presented in the next section.

FIVE GUIDELINES
FOR THE REFORMULATION

The Social Security program as presently set up clearly requires a major reformulation.

However, whatever changes are made must neither threaten the continued existence of the Social Security system itself nor severely impact the well being of present Social Security recipients or the companies and workers supporting them. Needless to say, it is equally important to prevent these reforms from threatening the overall national economy.

Although some reformers might wish to see a long and minutely detailed list providing a prescription for a reformulation, such an exhaustive list is neither desirable nor necessary. Such a list might be used as a back-door attempt to impose a certain preconceived plan. Instead, I believe most people prefer only a few basic guidelines which all rational people seeking reform could accept as **reasonable, just,** and **necessary** in any reformulation, while allowing for a variety of alternatives. If reasonable, just, and necessary are accepted as the standard, the only absolutely essential requirements are those given below:

First: Sustainability -- A way must be devised immediately to meet the spiraling expenses of Social

Security as the 77 million "Baby Boomers" reach retirement age. The steadily increasing numbers of new retirees becomes a major torrent beginning in 2008 as the wave of post-World War II babies reach age 62 and millions of them apply for benefits. Through their elected representatives over the years, the American people have made certain promises. Like all pledges made by Congress, not only must these promises be honored in the present, but legislation must be enacted that will insure their observance in the future. Any reforms adopted must not only assure an adequate income to meet the immediate expenditures for the flood of workers entering the ranks of retirees in the near future but also must generate increasingly greater amounts of revenue in the years ahead. Any proposed changes must recognize and plan for these long term, continuing increases to guarantee Social Security's **Sustainability.**

Second: Equity -- Children at a very young age learn that a valid objection that can be raised to any proposal is "That's not fair !". The Pledge of Allegiance, with which we are all familiar, in a similar vein ends with the promise of "justice for all". While all of us hope for fairness in every piece of legislation passed by Congress, we particularly want equity in taxing programs whose burdens are imposed now but whose benefits will not appear until decades in the future.

Compromises had to be made to meet the political realities of 1935. The well-off had just been hit with what was described as a "soak the rich" tax. Adding yet another new tax on their relatively large paychecks might appear as excessive and vindictive. So, as a workable compromise, a limit was placed on the amount of pay which would be taxed for a person's retirement (initially $3000, a fairly significant sum in 1935), but (in return) a poorer paid worker would be given a better payback on his "contribution" than that given his better paid fellow-employee.

The unfairness of not taxing a person's entire paycheck was recognized (but not fully addressed) when Medicare was added to the Social Security program in 1964. Since the Social Security tax at the time was bringing in enough income to pay the retirees' regular benefits, it was not felt necessary to raise the issue of eliminating the cap on wages at that time, and a compromise was arranged which would offset the predicted added expense. To pay the cost of the NEW benefit, a NEW tax of 1.45% was imposed on ALL WAGES of the employee (matched by their employer) with no upper limit.

Both those presently working and paying Social Security taxes and those retired and receiving payments could benefit from devising a more equitable means of financing retirement, Medicare, and the drug benefit. But, such equity in any reform can only be achieved if political parties and pressure groups avoid pitting one group's needs against another's wishes, turning Social Security reform into a win-lose rivalry.

Groups composed primarily of older Americans demand more benefits for retirees (such as having Medicare assume the cost for hearing aids, eye glasses, and long term care) while spreading fear among their members of a raid upon the Social Security Trust Fund, a "collapse of Social Security", the loss of Medicare, and a slashing of all benefits. NONSENSE! Benefits are paid by Congressionally authorized annual expenditures, and

Congress can and will add general revenue to the income from Social Security taxation if that ever become necessary to maintain full retiree benefits, just as is being done right now to sustain Medicare and the new prescription drug benefits. Reform must not involve a loss of benefits to those already retired.

On the other hand, labor groups warn their members Social Security taxes will balloon, extracting incredible sums from their paycheck unless they contact their Congressman and Senators, threatening them with voting booth retaliation. Young workers cynically assert (with typical youthful surety) that Social Security will go broke long before they retire, and they will receive no return on their taxes, while secretly hoping they're wrong. MORE NONSENSE !

Most members of Congress realize the Social Security tax of 7.65 % could not be raised to the levels necessary to fully fund all retiree benefits. A new, more equitable way must be found.

All Americans must be kept in mind when crafting Social Security's improvement. If done properly, the necessary reforms afford an opportunity to establish a greater degree of **equity.** Any reformulation of a program covering nearly all American citizens must have as its basis the ideal that all Americans will share jointly the burdens and benefits of Social Security.

Third: Comprehensiveness -- While old age retirement payments have always been considered at the heart of the Social Security program, its other provisions (of unemployment compensation, permanent disability payments, survivor's benefits, the various public assistance and education programs, Medicare, Medicaid, and the recently added prescription drug plans) are equally important. The scope and coverage of Social Security must not be whittled away bit by bit in a vain attempt to maintain its basic solvency. As its name implies, the Social Security program is designed to afford America's workers and their families comprehensive security against the social harms inevitable in modern society, just as the nation's military program protects them from external dangers.

Indeed, initiatives to improve the living conditions of the aging citizen must be considered. Instead of being forced to totally deplete their life long savings and being sent (frequently against their wishes) to retirement homes or forced to move in with relatives (creating considerable friction), seniors should be able to access programs such as Meals on Wheels, Independent Transportation Networks (providing drivers for the elderly who have lost or given up their drivers' licenses), live-in companions, emergency call systems, or home care companies providing weekly visits from nurses or physical therapists to guarantee their security and care while allowing them to retain their independence and remain within their own homes and familiar neighborhoods as long as possible. Assisted living housing, which affords differing levels of care according to the person's degree of mobility, independence, and medical condition, have proven a blessing for many elderly people. Hospice offers thousands a more humane and far less costly way to receive care when hospitals are not longer curative but only palliative. Such alternative programs are often expensive to set up, but usually provide significant savings later.

But, far more important than the savings realized, adding these innovative programs create a more fully **Comprehensive** system for both working and retired citizens.

Fourth: Predictability -- As far as is humanly possible, the timing and extent of any changes to the Social Security program must be made totally predictable.

The stock market, businesses, and individuals fear nothing more than uncertainty. Entire industries, such as insurance companies, futurists, business consultants, and economic theorists (not to mention astrologers and fortune tellers), have grown up to predict and safeguard against looming dangers, permitting corporations and individuals to take corrective actions to offset potential disasters. Corporations and capital markets can adjust to even the most catastrophic situation if its advent is clearly and precisely predictable.

Employers, workers, and the general public need to be able to foresee the impact of Social Security on their lives years in the future. Large and small enterprises have to be able to accurately estimate the new expenses of Social Security when negotiating with employees and arranging long term contracts with upper management. Employees need to know how much they will pay, how much they can expect to receive when they retire, and how much of their retirement expenses they'll need to finance some other way. The general public must be able to calculate the hidden cost of Social Security taxation as an added expense on items they are planning to purchase.

Alterations in a program involving billions of dollars annually as well as impacting the life and welfare of nearly every retiree, employer, and working person and his family can and ought be explained fully and clearly in advance, and as closely as possible, the changes must be implemented exactly as stated, insuring a high degree of **Predictability.**

Fifth: Economically Helpful -- Any program reformulation needs to strengthen the American economy. Instead of allowing 77 million retirees (and the latest wave of economic and social changes the "baby boomers" have wrought at every stage of their aging) to become a drag on the economy or a threat to other generations, carefully crafted legislation can convert unavoidable alteration into economic advantage.

Already, agile companies, aware of the tremendous opportunities provided by a market of fairly affluent older citizens, offer "age adjusted" housing (with less floor level storage areas, safety bars pre-installed for bath tubs, seats in showers, and wider hallways accommodating wheel chairs or walkers), fold out step assists and swivel seats in automobiles (to aid entry and exiting), cruises featuring "big band" musical programs or the aged "stars" of 1950's pop music, medication to ease the multitude of problems accompanying aging, and retirement communities offering varying levels of care adapted to the person's abilities and needs. The list could be extended and will grow even more as marketers see new opportunities.

Even local communities and states are redesigning themselves to be seen as "retirement friendly" (since older people do not require the building of new schools, bring Medicare and retirement money to finance state programs, and seldom rob banks or engage in other violent crimes).

With an aging population and an increasing number of retirees, the willingness of the older generation to spend will prove vital to sustaining the economy. Maintaining a sense of economic security among the elderly (which may encourage them to spend more freely) without imposing a huge burden upon the working population (whose spending is equally vital to the American economy) is possible with a balanced plan. The changing needs of a growing and aging population offers immense opportunities, provided the money is not taken from the younger generation – and it need not be. Balancing the desires of retirees with the needs of present day workers can prove **Economically Helpful** to the nation.

Following the five guidelines given above (**Sustainability, Equity, Comprehensiveness,**

Predictability, and **Economically Helpful**), Congress can craft programs that will not only solve the "problem" of Social Security long term but also will allow its revitalization in the 21st Century. Although the Plano Plan focuses primarily on financing, there is no reason these same guidelines ought not be employed when considering suggested reformulations in other aspects of Social Security as well.

The next sections offer five specific suggestions for Social Security reform, along with an examination of the rationale for the adoption of each, how they can be incorporated gradually into the existing system, and how well they conform with the five principles given above.

Eliminating the Cap on Earnings Taxed

The single most important feature of the Plano Plan (and, indeed, the one feature that is absolutely indispensable in any realistic plan designed to make Social Security both sustainable and equitable) is elimination of the cap on earnings subject to Social Security taxation.

As pointed out earlier, Social Security is in essence just another TAX. Calling Social Security's weekly exaction a payment on some sort of employment insurance, a health insurance policy for later life, or a "contribution" to a special government retirement program doesn't make it anything other than a TAX. This tax is "special" or "unique" only in one way – the worst way. It is, by far, the most unfairly regressive tax in the United States.

As the law is presently written, every wage earner pays 6.2% of the first $94,200 of his earnings into the retirement portion. In addition, every worker pays 1.45% of his entire earnings (regardless of the amount) into Social Security for Medicare. The total of these two amounts is matched by his employer. If the person is self-employed, he is obligated to pay both the employee and the employer amounts (since he is both), or 12.4 % of his first $94,200 for retirement and 2.9% of his entire earnings for

Medicare. Thus, an employee who earns exactly $94,200 pays $1,365.90 for Medicare along with an additional $5,840.40 for retirement, or a total of $7,206.30 every year, an effective tax rate of 7.65 %. This sum is matched by his employer (or, if he is self-employed, the sum is doubled).

However, when the person's salary climbs above the $94,200 level, the system which up to that point appears very rational and just, becomes totally unreasonable and outrageously unfair.

Let's assume some employee earns ten times the cap amount, with the income used for figuring his retirement "contribution" now $942,000 (rather than $94,200). While still obliged to pay 1.45% for Medicare (which now totals $13,659), he is exempt from paying anything additional into the retirement account (which remains at $5840.40). His ten-fold advantage in pay earns him a 90% REDUCTION in the taxes he pays for retirement. His actual tax rate for the Social Security retirement portion falls from 6.2% to a mere 0.62 %. If his Medicare portion is included, his actual effective tax rate for Medicare and retirement declines from 7.65% to a mere 2.07%, or a 73% lower rate than that exacted from his less well paid colleague.

If an employee's earnings climb to a princely $ 9,420,000 (or 100 times the cap imposed on Social Security retirement taxes), the amount paid for retirement remains unchanged ($5,840.40), lowering his tax rate for the retirement portion to a paltry 0.062% (or 1/16 of 1%). Even with the payment for Medicare (now $136,590) added on, his total effective Social Security tax rate shrivels to a mere 1.5%.

THE MORE A PERSON EARNS, THE LOWER HIS SOCIAL SECURITY TAX RATE !

By definition, such a tax is regressive. By any standard of morality, it is grossly unjust ! Sustainability and simple basic equity demand spreading the increasing burden of Social Security more fairly among all workers.

Although the obvious, regressive-eliminating solution is simply to remove the cap on earnings and tax the entire amount, as is already done with the Medicare portion of Social Security, compelling reasons exist for not removing it immediately.

The economic effect of any such sudden tax increase would be catastrophic to both businesses and to the individuals faced with the massive tax increase. Business plans by large corporations would have to be rethought and projects delayed, with funds instead redirected to handle this sudden, unexpected, massive new expenditure. Huge amounts of corporate money would have to be withdrawn (or, at least, withheld) from money markets to cover the following year's Social Security required matching of workers' payments. The tax increase on individual employees would impact retailers by disrupting the spending patterns of millions of buyers facing a sudden decrease in income. Its impact would ripple across the national economy.

Fortunately, these difficulties can be eliminated by the gradual, fully predictable (and finally total) removal of the cap on earnings. Just as a football team that falls behind by 20 points cannot expect to recover the lead with one simple series of plays, this regressive and unjust tax feature cannot be corrected immediately. The football team focuses on preventing the deficit from growing any worse, while getting to work on the much more important goal, which is coming up with a plan to retake the lead or at least reaching the point where that can be done in one play, well before the final minutes of the game adds new urgency to its task. Likewise, Congress must focus on its dual tasks: Ultimately completely removing the injustice and working toward that goal at a rapid pace.

Congress has already taken the first steps by authorizing an annual rise in the amount of earnings subject to taxation for the retirement fund. Under the present law, the cap on earnings has been gradually increasing on a yearly basis by several thousand a year, to reflect the increase in average wages. But the amounts are far too small, the schedule far too long, and the basic inequity untouched.

Because the arrival of large numbers of "Baby Boomers" at retirement age is imminent, the major corrections must be made swiftly – at most in a decade or two, not in a century or "someday" (which seems to be the present plan).

In addition, while the present law appears to be reform, this "reform" actually made the inequity even worse. Such a glacial pace of increase simply cannot keep pace with recent compensation packages given to top corporate executives which are accelerating at a supersonic pace (thus DECREASING still further their actual tax rate over the past two decades). The law now seems to imply that only the "super-rich" deserve the Social Security Tax Benefit – only those earning over $100,000 need the decreased level of taxation ! In 19th Century France, the right to vote was conditional upon payment of a certain amount of taxes. When reformers called for expanding the franchise, the finance minister (Francois Guizot) is reported to have retorted that everyone was equally free to grow rich and secure the vote. Today, our Congress similarly is stating, "If you want to lower your Social Security taxes, get super rich !"

Simple revisions could accelerate the size and pace of the increases and in one or two decades completely eliminate the cap. The gradual and predictable nature of the increase would allow corporate accountants to anticipate and factor in the increases as they draw up projections for future years. As years pass and the present top executives move into retirement, the Board of Directors and a prospective new CEO or COO would bargain with the predictable, gradually increasing cap a factor in negotiations. Corporate Boards might choose to slowly rein in the size of "bonuses" and "incentives" awarded or offer new corporate top officers somewhat smaller initial salaries. Prospective officers might have to adjust the amounts requested to reflect the long term impact of Social Security taxation upon their prospective employers and their own compensations. All workers could see the significant increases and the promise of the cap's total elimination by a definite date.

The yearly increase ought be restrained in the first few years, further weakening its impact on the economy. For example, the first yearly increase from $94,200 to $125,000 would not be a cataclysmic, since most of those covered by the new cap are probably already at $94,200. The new expenditure is not 7.65 % of $125,000 (or $9,562.50), but only the difference between that figure and what is already paid ($7206 under the present schedule). For large companies, the additional $2,356.50 per year for middle level executives is easily manageable, while smaller companies probably have few (if any) employees at the higher pay level. An executive earning $125,000 or more has enough discretionary income to handle his tax increase without a drastic alteration of his lifestyle.

Over a period not to exceed two decades, the cap could safely be raised from $94,200 to an unlimited sum. Each annual increase would impact increasing larger pay checks, but since the changes would affect increasingly fewer employees (since few receive extremely large pay checks), the actual increase in tax revenue, while steady, would not be huge in any one year. But, over time, the taxes paid on these higher salaries would increase the amount coming into the Social Security fund, insuring additional funding to pay future retirement benefits and helping to defray the rising expenses of Medicare and prescription drugs. **

Financially, removing the cap is prudent. Morally, it is imperative.

Some may contend this is a back-door tax increase or a soak the rich scheme (a charge which led the Roosevelt Administration to insert an earnings cap in the original law since it had just influenced Congress to increase taxes on the well off). However, I would contend that removing the cap ought not be viewed this way. If I receive a special tax break and Congress chooses to eliminate that break, I cannot legitimately object that this as a tax increase. The law is merely eliminating a previously extended tax break.

In fact, such tax readjustments are relatively routine. When the Individual Retirement Accounts were introduced in the 1980's, every wage earner was allowed to deduct from his income tax up to $2000 deposited in a special IRA certified account. This special tax break was designed to encourage wage earners to save and set aside money for their eventual retirement. But it worked too well, causing federal revenues to plummet. The law was "adjusted" to limit IRA tax deductions to certain lower income individuals for whom post-retirement Social Security payments alone would not provide financial security. This amendment, like the reform for removing the cap on earnings, cannot be considered a tax increase on those affected. Rather, it is the removal of a special tax benefit granted previously to a select few.

How well does this change square with the five principles listed in the last section ?

Obviously, the long term **Sustainability** of Social Security is substantially improved. The slow but steadily increasing flow of funds into the program will allow continuation of the pay-as-you-go principle that has been a feature of the program since its inception. The major difference is that the creators of the program envisioned an increasingly larger labor force whose payments would provide income for a very limited number of retirees for the short period between retirement and death. Today's reform must envision a relatively stable or decreasing number of workers supporting an increasingly larger number of retirees over a much longer period of time. Removing the cap on wages guarantees all wage earners will support those already retired (as they themselves can expect to be supported when they retire).

Willie Sutton (a famous or infamous, but not terribly successful bank robber) was asked why he continued robbing banks. His reply was "Because that's where the money is !" Similarly, Social Security must go where the money is. Social Security cannot maintain the pay-as-you-go principle if it taxes merely the lowest paid wage earners while ignoring the highest paid employees. Only by having all workers paying the same percentage (though different dollar amounts) can the original idea of pay-as-you-go be maintained.

As with sustainability, the **Equity** is so obvious little needs to be said about it. To demand that the employee receiving lower wages pay a larger portion of his lesser income in taxes is an idea so preposterous that it need hardly be addressed. Even a child could plainly see, "That's not fair!" Congress, representing and acting in the name of all the citizens of the United States, promised 70 years ago to help older Americans maintain their dignity and independence following retirement by having all working people make small monthly payments to them. A promise of basic medical care was added in 1964, and still later a pledge of limited assistance in obtaining prescription medicine. Since these promises were made on behalf of all the citizens, those same citizens are equally bound to finance it by giving an equal PERCENTAGE of their income during their working careers.

This provision also shows a commitment to the concept that no group shall be asked to bear an undue imposition to reform Social Security. The burden now will be more fairly distributed among all workers based upon their earnings. Those earning the most will, of course, pay the largest amount, but their percentage will be identical to everyone else's. Since a larger income results in a great amount of discretionary income, the extra payments will not significantly weaken their ability to continue enjoying the good life.

Removing the cap on wages allows Social Security to become more **Comprehensive**. The slow but steadily increasing flow of money from Social Security payroll taxes (along with the other reforms suggested by the Plano Plan) will insure that no additional large taxes increases need be imposed to support the increasing numbers and needs of an aging population. Receiving more income, Social Security can continue paying retirement pensions and still have enough revenue to gradually assume more of the rising cost of Medicare and prescription drugs, assisting Congress in its search for new ways to care for the increasing number of elderly in ever tighter budgets. Its income more certain, Medicare may even be able to expand the types of services it can provide without imposing large premium increases.

As stressed above, **Predictability** is essential for preventing disruption in the economy as the cap on wages is removed. The increased cost for companies required to match the taxes paid by their employees is easily computed when these additional expenses are explicitly indicated in advance and, along with other expenses, are totally predictable in the short term. While inflation, the cost of capital, increasing wages, and other factors may distort long term predictions in many areas, the precise statements of the amount and timing of the increased expenses for Social Security would allow business to plan and preposition money for the added expense.

Finally, removing the cap is **Helpful to the Economy.** Older citizens, assured that their monthly pensions are not in jeopardy of being decreased by 30% as Social Security reserves run dry, will be more willing to spend on discretionary items, putting more money into the economy and more sales taxes into state treasuries. Agile companies will continue their increased marketing to the elderly and invent new items that make their lives easier or allow them to continue living on their own for a much longer period. The spending by this group is not inconsequential. In 2000, the percentage of citizens over 65 was 12.4 %; by 2030, they are expected to form 20% of the U.S. population.

But elimination of the cap on earnings must not be seen as a once step cure for the problems facing Social Security. This increase in funding is absolutely essential but not sufficient on its own to render secure the program's long term financing. As mentioned parenthetically above, the Plano Plan includes other features. These other additional features are detailed the sections that follow.

** If a more precise schedule is demanded from me, I would suggest something like the following:

Year	Increase to	Year	Increase to	Year	Increase to
1st	125,000	8th	400,000	15th	1,000,000
2nd	150,000	9th	475,000	16th	2,000,000
3rd	175,000	10th	550,000	17th	4,000,000
4th	200,000	11th	625,000	18th	6,000,000
5th	250,000	12th	700,000	19th	8,000,000
6th	300,000	13th	800,000	20th	Uncapped
7th	350,000	14th	900.000		

The basic idea is to make the increases small at the start but increasing steadily in size:

$25,000 in the first four years; $50,000 in the next four years; $75,000 in the next four, and $100,000 in a final group of three. The increases, though significantly larger in AMOUNT in the final six years of the schedule, have a SMALLER impact because of the wealthier person's relatively greater discretionary income. The small increases may produce a shortfall in some of the middle years, but eventually they should be able to fully cover the retirement benefits and a significant portion of other benefits as well, especially if the other suggested Plano Plan reforms are adopted.

Readjusting the Monthly Retirement Payments

Although removing the cap on earnings alone would be a major step in restoring equity, guaranteeing the sustainability, and eventually extending the comprehensiveness of Social Security, additional changes are necessary. Greater sustainability and equity can be attained by altering the way monthly benefits paid retirees are determined and creating a two-tiered system for granting automatic annual increases.

Under the present system an individual's retirement benefits are determined primarily by two factors:

The first of these two factors is totally outside the person's control: His parents and the community in which he is raised. It has been correctly stated that no baby can pick his parents, but the baby born to parents who are rich (or, at least, relatively well off) enjoys a great advantage throughout his life. If a child's parents are wealthy and live in a community that is willing to financially support high quality schools, public libraries, museums, playgrounds, and cultural attractions, the child has a head start from the beginning. When parents are well-educated and realize the advantages offered by a comprehensive, quality education, they fill their home with books, computers, and educational toys, encourage their child to do well in school, and make sure the child receives instruction in music, foreign languages, computers, mathematics, and science. They enroll their child in special summer camps and sometimes even hire private tutors (when needed). Family vacations to historic national monuments or parks are easily within the family budget. The child's parents insure he can afford to attend the "right college" and be offered a position with a prestigious firm through family connections and neighborhood networks.

Of course, the child may have other advantages unique to him, such as a high I.Q., a lively curiosity, inventiveness, an inspiring teacher or coach that recognizes and nurtures his particular talents, or an astute friend who guides him through a maze of financial opportunities. This also is mostly outside his control: just luck.

The second factor in determining a person's retirement payments is what the child (and later the adult) adds to his initial endowment. The child must be willing to study hard to master subjects or acquire competencies that will bring him a good income. The lure of the playground or the immediate pay offered by jobs that require less skill is spurned for additional years in the college classroom or at graduate school. Summer classes chosen over time at the beach and weekend sessions to get the necessary certification and advancement in a profession generally mean more pay (and thus greater retirement benefits). Dedication and decisions add to what comes from luck.

Thus, under the present system, the size of a person's retirement benefits is based partly on luck and partly on pluck. The amount of his retirement allowance is determined by the total amount of Social Security taxes a person pays during his working career (reflecting his average monthly earnings on which Social Security is paid). Retirement payment adjustments are made for those retiring either earlier or later than the present standard retirement age of 66. Those who, earning more, pay a greater amount into the system (albeit the same percentage until the $94,200 ceiling is reached) receive a greater monthly benefit when they retire. Regardless of the amount paid in Social Security taxes, all covered workers are enrolled in Medicare at age 65.

Making the system more just, the law already provides a higher percentage of benefits for each dollar collected for those workers receiving a lesser average pay over their working years. This is recognition of the fact that lower skilled workers, seasonal workers, irregularly employed household workers, and those voluntarily accepting lower pay (such as teachers, clergymen, members of religious orders, and workers in private social service groups) provide valuable and necessary contributions to the society and deserve some financial recompense for the labor done for lower pay when they retire. Survivors and dependents of those covered by Social Security also receive substantial benefits to insure their well being.

Although an imbalance still remains (with the highest paid employees still receiving greater monthly payments), this method helps to make more equitable the monthly payments given to Social Security recipients. For example, the monthly sum awarded to a couple whose Social Security taxes were at the maximum earning level would be just below $ 2500. By comparison, a couple who earned pay at the lowest level (an amount less than 45% of the average earnings level) receive less than half as much in monthly payments (even when their benefits are calculated using a larger multiplier). Additional adjustments are made for children under 18 in a family where the primary wage earner dies (with the amount paid relative to what the covered person would have received at retirement). Thus, a widowed mother or father with dependent children may be eligible for monthly payments totaling nearly $ 3000.

In addition to these basic payments, Congress provides for an annual automatic cost of living adjustment beginning in December of each year, designed to counter the eroding effects of inflation on the purchasing power of the retired person. The increase in the monthly payments is determined by the percentage rise in the Consumer Price Index between the third quarter of one year and the third quarter of the directly preceding year.

However, despite these attempts at fairness, a basic inequity does remain. Awarding a life-long worker lesser benefits because he paid less in taxes is basically unjust. If I am an extremely wealthy person and thus pay a huge amount in income taxes every year, I have no right to demand that the Defense Department station a platoon of soldiers in my back yard and install a surface-to-air missile battery at the end of my street to better protect me. Rather, my taxes are pooled with those of my less affluent neighbors and countrymen to provide for our common defense. The fact I pay more taxes reflects my greater earnings, and I may not demand greater protection because of my higher tax payments. Likewise, if my job brings me a greater income, I ought not expect a greater return for my tax payment than someone who pays less.

An even more serious problem will arise as the cap on earnings is gradually phased out if the present formula used for determining benefits is retained. Some Social Security tax payers (those receiving multi-million dollar salaries) would be awarded enormous month benefits upon their retirement.

Happily the solution to this problem is obvious: a cap must be installed on the monthly benefits paid any retiree. However, because promises of benefits have been given and those promises must be honored, the cap placed on future benefits must be equal to or greater than the highest monthly payments presently given any retiree. The present formulation can be retained, but the monthly benefit awarded in the future will be the amount determined by the formula OR the amount set by the cap, whichever is less. Since the original cap set on payments is equal to or greater than any benefits presently being paid, no one would see a lowering of his monthly check. The cap would be raised annually to reflect increases in the Consumer Price Index.

But promising that benefit increases in the future will be of equal size for all is required neither by equity nor by common sense.

Rather, what is required is a gradual, predictable plan for providing larger monthly benefit payments to those who need them most, taking into consideration the income of a retiree from all sources.

Despite impressive gains over the past few decades, the percentage of retired people at or below the poverty level remains significant, especially among certain groups. The poverty rate for all people over 65 is approximately 10%, but the rate for African-Americans over 65 is 15.6%. For African-American women over 65, the percentage climbs to 25%.

Happily, a partial remedy (suggested by an economist and immediately embraced by President Bush) has been proposed. Those above the average monthly benefit payment level would receive an annual increase equal to the previous year's rate of inflation, while those at or below the average would receive an annual increase equal to the prior year's increase in the cost of living (which is presently given to all retirees). The annual Cost of Inflation increase would offset the eroding effect of inflation for those at the top, while those below the average would continue to receive Cost of Living increases to meet their rising living expenses. Such a modification not only recognizes the role a person's luck played in determining for him a better or lesser position and wages, but also rewards the pluck which allowed him to use whatever endowment he had to the greatest advantage (or, conversely, his willingness to make a personal sacrifice for the benefit of others).

Two modifications ought to be considered with regard to this proposal. First, a cap must be placed on the maximum annual increases allowable due to inflation or a rise in the cost of living. Were inflation to reappear at the horrendous rates experienced in the 1970's, its impact on the Social Security could quickly become catastrophic. A maximum 8 % increase in the Cost of Inflation and a 50 % higher figure (12 %) on the Cost of Living should prove sufficient to protect the older person's buying power while safeguarding the long-term viability of Social Security despite a sudden spike in the inflation rate. Hopefully, prompt intervention in the financial markets by the federal government using a variety of tested techniques would preclude the need to ever use these caps.

A second possible modification would be to use 150% of the poverty level as the dividing line between those receiving the Cost of Inflation rather than the Cost of Living increase. Several economists have pointed to an increasing gap between the highest paid and lowest paid workers in the American corporations (even worst than that so evident in the 1890's and early 1900's). The high poverty levels among the elderly (noted above) might over time be ameliorated somewhat by using the poverty index for determining Social Security increases. (Incidentally, this would also provide a way to measure our progress in successfully eliminating poverty among the elderly.)

This reform, like the previous one, needs to be measured against the standards given in the introduction.

The plan would decrease the annual expenditures for Social Security, adding another component to insure its **Sustainability**. Under the present system, all retirees receive the cost of living increase. Under the proposed revision some (but fewer) continue receiving the cost of living increase, while the remainder receive the lower cost of inflation increases. This reformulation alone would never be able to offset the new expenditures required for the 77 million new "Baby Boomer" retirees, but the savings would be significant enough (along with other reforms) to allow the program to continue without any decrease in benefits to retirees (since all receive some sort of annual increase) or any rise in the Social Security tax presently imposed on workers and employers.

As was indicated above, although the plan does not offers complete parity in monthly payments either immediately or at any time in the future, it provides greater **Equity** than now exists. All (both workers and retirees) are sharing equally the burdens and benefits. No worker pays higher Social Security taxes (unless his tax is increased due to the rising cap on earnings), and no retiree loses any benefits he already has. Although some would experience a decline in the size of their automatic annual adjustment, all receive annual increases to maintain their buying power. Those who enjoy a greater retirement income from their hard work, wise planning, or conscientiousness (values which ought not be discouraged) continue to receive protection of their buying power by an annual increase equal to the cost of inflation. Those having the least retirement income and most in need of an increase to maintain their buying power receive the larger cost of living increase. Obviously, if this greater percentage succeeds in pushing the person above 150% of the poverty level, in the following years he receives the cost of inflation adjustment instead.

As with the earlier reform, the savings experienced could help offset the constantly rising costs of Medicare, Medicaid, and the Social Security Insurance Programs (unemployment, survivors, and disability insurance). These savings further insure that Social Security will continue to provide **Comprehensive** coverage to all workers and all retirees.

The plan has as great a **Predictability** as exists under the present system. No one can accurately predict the future of the Consumer Price Index, which triggers the automatic cost of living increase, but the monthly and quarterly reports issued near the start of each fiscal year (in October) allow early estimates of expenditures for the following year. Thus, the same degree of predictability would exist as is possible now. In addition, the limits placed on the Cost of Living and Cost of Inflation increases would allow economists to compute "worst case" estimates well before the start of the next fiscal year.

Whether or not the plans would be **Helpful to the Economy** is hard to predict. While the change might lead to a downturn in spending by some at the highest level (who might decrease their spending to conserve funds) and such a decline in spending would be harmful, spending by those at the lower levels would continue (since much of the spending is for necessities) probably more than offsetting the decline. More likely, spending by both those at the higher and those at the lower levels would continue basically unchanged.

Although raising the cap on earnings which are taxed and adjusting how benefits are paid out are frequently recognized as ways of aiding the survival of Social Security, two other ways exist to increase the amount of money available for the program. These components are detailed in the next two sections.

RAISING THE AGE FOR RETIREMENT

Reformulating Social Security by eliminating the cap on wages subject to taxation and creating a two-tiered system for automatic annual benefit adjustments are major steps toward correcting the long range financing problems confronting Social Security. However, a third part of the system based on the assumptions of 1935 (which subsequently proved incorrect) must be reconsidered and revised. While both logical and essential, adjusting the age at which a person becomes eligible to receive Social Security monthly retirement payments may prove the most contentious of all issues that must be addressed when reformulating Social Security.

When the Social Security program was first created for American workers, the plan basically duplicated the provisions included in the original system of social insurance drawn up by Chancellor Otto von Bismarck for German workers in the 1880's. Following this 19th Century German model closely, America's Social Security provided insurance against long-term disabling illnesses or accidents, survivors' benefits, matching payments by workers and their employers, and a retirement age of 65. That retirement age had been selected by a nameless

German bureaucrat who decided at 65 a worker was so mentally and physically decrepit he was no longer able to carry out his tasks in a factory or to perform any other worth-while labor for wages.

Congress, fully aware the life expectancy of a person in the United States in 1935 was 62 years, nevertheless readily adopted the figure used in the German system. The Congressmen and Senators concluded that most workers would never receive retirement benefits, and the few who did would get them for only a short time. The Roosevelt Administration included the workmen's coverage and survivors' benefits from the German package as an added inducement for Congressional approval. The worker, though unlikely to recoup any of the money he had set aside for his age 65 retirement, would also be buying protection against his own unemployment or disability, the destitution of his family if he died before retirement, and the total loss of income by his wife and minor children following his death.

But, things have changed a great deal since then 1935 , and Social Security was not altered to reflect those changes. The American in the 21st Century has a average life expectancy in excess of 77 years, and those reaching 65 years of age have a better than even chance of surviving to age 85. As pointed out earlier, people aged 65 or older made up 12.4 % of the population in 2000, but the United States Bureau of Census estimates that figure will grow to 20 % (or 70 million) by 2030.

When the opportunity to retire at age 62 (with reduced benefits) was introduced in the 1950's, many workers took advantage of that new provision, adding millions to the retired population and several years to the length of time they would receive benefits. As the 2000 census figures show, the percentage of people aged 62-64 already receiving Social Security retirement benefits was 53% (although a large number in that age range [64%] were fully able to continue working part time and earn additional income from wages and salaries).

As the large percentage of part-time workers between 62 and 65 shows, the worker's general fitness for employment extends to a later age due to better sanitation, widespread state-sponsored hygiene programs, universal vaccination plans, more advanced medical and rehabilitation treatments, and better quality, fresher, and generally healthier foods. Mandated health and safety programs not only cut substantially the number of fatal accidents and major injuries incurred at work but also protected workers from the dangers and long term consequences of hazardous working conditions.

At the same time, the physical strength required from employees has decreased markedly in many occupations. Factories, which formerly needed strong, young (mostly male) workers to move, lift, carry, or drag heavy objects, now employ conveyor belts, electricity, and fork lifts, reducing the effort required from human muscle. Office work has become less strenuous and body numbing by the extensive use of bright lighting, air-conditioning, ergonomically designed equipment, and computers (which allow frequently sent documents, requiring only minor alterations, to be quickly personalized, modified, and printed without extensive repetitious retyping).

The combined results of these changes are dramatic. The worker of today is now likely not only to receive some retirement benefits but also to receive them for many years and far in excess of the amount he paid in Social Security taxes (even when interest on that taxation is added). Many workers, including almost all of the 77 million Baby-Boomers and even if they retire with reduce benefits at 62, will receive more retirement payments in five to six years than they paid in 40 or more years of work. Since the average life expectancy is 77 (and even higher for those reaching 62), some retirees' benefits may exceed their tax payments by better than three to one.

Further complicating the problem, the ratio of workers (benefit payers) to retirees (benefit receivers) is constantly shrinking, from an estimated high of 40 to 1 when Social Security was originally set up to less than 3 to 1 today. Projections show a further slippage to 2 to 1 (by around 2030) as the vast number of Baby-Boomers move into retirement. Absolute parity (when the number of retirees equals the number of workers supporting them) has already appeared in some industries, such as automobile manufacturing. These declining ratios are not due to a decrease in the number of workers. Rather, it reflects an increase in the number of employees reaching retirement and their lengthening post-retirement life-span.

Obviously, such ratios are simply unsustainable. The financial strain placed upon workers to provide adequate benefits both for themselves and for all retirees, especially when retirement extends over an ever increasing number of years, will eventually become too great. Eliminating the cap on wages taxed and different annual adjustments in benefit payments would help ease the strain to a great extent in the future. But if Congress resists both these changes and insists on retaining the present Social Security financing system on a pay as you go basis, only a drastic rise in the taxes paid by the workers and matched by their employers or a catastrophic cut in benefits to retirees could provide enough revenue. As pointed out earlier, the Social Security "reserve" is illusory. Using general revenue to fill the gap would devastate other necessary programs, create an unsustainable National Debt (already requiring almost $400 BILLION per year in interest alone), and irreparably harm the economy.

The present Social Security system provides a hint about what must be done to create a more reasonable age of retirement. The three tiered system of reduced benefits, normal benefits, and enhanced benefits can be retained but needs to be raised to more reasonable levels and needs to be implemented more quickly than is presently provided for in law. Under the present law, the full benefits retirement age crawls slowly upward from 65 to 67 --- registering the final phase in of age 67 in 2027! This, of course, ignores the fact that well over 1/2 of today's retirees have begun taking reduced benefits at age 62 (while continuing to work part time). Unless the minimum age for receiving any retirement benefits is increased, raising the age for receiving normal benefits or enhanced benefits is superfluous.

Raising the retirement age in all three tiers by three months per year for the next 12 to 20 years would reduce Social Security's total monthly payments to more acceptable levels by postponing the point at which new retirees first receive monthly benefit payments and decreasing the total number of years during which they get retirement pensions. The age for reduced benefits would rise from 62 to 65 (over a 12 year period), allowing an early retirement for those who plan carefully, save wisely, or can decrease their expenses during retirement. The age for full benefits would rise from its present 66 to 70 years of age (over 16 years), perhaps making 70 the new common age for retirement. Enhanced benefits would begin at 75 years of age (reached over a 20 year period), which might be chosen by those who enjoy their jobs or who realize they could still expect over a decade and a half of life after retirement. If this, along with the other alterations suggested earlier, are implemented soon enough, any decrease in benefits can be avoided.

Under this system, no one presently receiving Social Security retirement benefits would lose them. Since the levels would rise slowly and fully predictably over 20 years or less at three months per year, those close to retirement would have adequate time to adjust. For example, a person within four years of retirement would have to plan for one additional year of employment --- which is not unduly burdensome. Those farther from retirement would find the adjustment easier still.

Significant savings would result from these changes in retirement ages. In 2005, the Social Security Administration paid out $ 574 billion in benefits. Presently about 50 cents of every dollar spent by the federal government – or approximately ONE TRILLION DOLLARS yearly -- goes to a retired person (including Social Security, Medicare, Veterans' benefits, and the government employee pensions). As noted above, almost half of all workers are choosing to collect benefits at the reduced level (age 62), a figure that is likely to increase.

Just delaying benefit payments by three years would result in significant savings. But additional substantial benefits to the economy result from healthy workers continuing their employment. If only a quarter of healthy people aged 65 to 75 remained in the work force, economists estimate the nation's economic output would increase by $350 billion per year. Goldman Sachs estimated that raising the retirement age to 70 would boost the Gross Domestic Product by 0.5 % and increase income levels by 11% over the next two decades.

Already major corporations, recognizing the value of their experienced workers, have instituted programs to retain those skilled employees by encouraging them to delay retirement. For example, one company allows workers to spend summers at their outlets in the cooler North, then move to Southern outlets in the colder months since the skills required are virtually identical in either area. Other companies allow less than full time work or flexible hours to fit individual schedules. Many high schools recruit retired science instructors or former administrators on a part time basis because adequately trained replacements are not available, while a substantial portion of community college and even four year college faculty are part-time, semi-retired ex-teachers or professors.

Objections to the older age for retirement can justly be raised by those in particularly dangerous, exhausting, or physically demanding labor (for example, mining, steel working, road construction, fire rescue, etc.) or those struggling with disabilities. But, most fields include supervisory or technical positions alongside those requiring heavy physical exertion. A worker can frequently move into a less strenuous position (supervising younger, less experienced employees) as age lessens his ability to perform the physical labor involved. If it chooses to do so, Congress could even authorize earlier benefit ages for particular, specifically enumerated jobs, or for work whose qualifying requirements indicate it demands such exertion.

Does this reform meet the guidelines listed earlier ?

The overall drop in annual expenditures for retirement will aid the **Sustainability** of the Social Security system. As the age of retirement move slowly upward, the number of workers entering the ranks of retirees yearly will decrease somewhat for a short period of time. While the overall amount of Social Security retirement payments will decrease only slightly if at all (due to the increasing number of living recipients), a decrease in the length of years over which benefits are paid will save significant amounts in the long run and sustain the level of payments for all retirees. In addition, as shown above, their continued employment would increase the Gross Domestic Product and increase the revenue obtained from Social Security taxation.

This proposal, like the earlier two, provides for greater **Equity** than the present system. As originally envisioned, Social Security was to be self-sustaining, with workers paying taxes to support those already retired, with future generations of workers paying to support them in their "golden years" when they themselves were too old to work. The original plan foresaw only a few short years following retirement (if the person lived to 65), not today's situation where a quarter of a person's life is spent in retirement. Since improvements in health and greater mechanization in the workplace have lengthened the number of years during which a person is capable of productive labor, eligibility for retirement should logically be postponed.

Equity requires this change to better balance the years of productive paid work with the years of enjoyable, earned, and financially and medically protected retirement. Although it undeniably does require the employee to increase his years of employment before retirement (but at most only three years for those planning retirement at 62 – now postponed to 65), the imposition of this extra burden cannot be considered unduly onerous or unfair.

To provide a **Comprehensive** program which takes into account particular unique situations which may affect retirement, Congress ought to recognize and delineate specifically in this reformulation those occupations where increased age would definitely be detrimental to productive labor (those imposing very strenuous physical tasks) and which provide no alternative employment roles with less physically demanding labor for the older workers. An earlier retirement age in those occupations is fully justified.

Absolute **Predictability** is possible with this part of the program, since the increases in all three levels are phased in at the same steady rate (three months per year). The worker, his employer, and Social Security can easily determine when the worker becomes eligible for retirement benefits and the amount he will receive (depending on the tier he selects).

Raising the age for retirement will also prove **Helpful to the Economy.** An employer is able to retain longer a skillful and experienced worker, whose wages are adding to the economy and whose Social Security taxes are providing additional income (instead of an expenditure) for the federal budget. As shown above, continuing employment for even a short period can be very beneficial to the overall economy (though exactly how helpful will depend on which tier the majority of workers select).

ADDING MEANS TESTING TO SOCIAL SECURITY

All the changes advocated of to this point have involved reformulations of the already existing features of the Social Security program to increase its income (by removing the cap on earnings taxed) or to decrease its expenditures (by setting a cap on retirement benefits with alternate automatic adjustment of benefits and by raising the age of retirement). A useful addition to the existing program to ensure its long term sustainability and comprehensiveness is means testing.

Although not intended to be so when the program was originally set up, Social Security has become for many retirees the sole or single most important component of their retirement income. A recent (July 2006) AARP Poll showed 28% of current retirees questioned had not saved any money for retirement during their working years, with 58% saying Social Security is a major source of their income. The poll concluded, "[M]any American workers may not have adjusted to the new economic reality … and many have not begun to save for the costs they'll face."

Social Security's retirement benefit was designed to be the third leg of the three legged stool for supporting the retired worker, supplementing the two traditional guarantees for post-employment financial security: personal savings and employer-provided pensions. Workers were counseled to prepare for their "golden years" while they were working by putting money safely aside in bank accounts (insured by the FDIC) or by purchasing the absolutely reliable United States Savings Bonds (through the Payroll Savings Plan which allowed workers to have money automatically deducted from their weekly pay checks to purchase bonds). Employers were encouraged to provide generous pension benefits (an item sure to be vigorously negotiated in every union contract and included in every executive's pay package). Social Security would become the final component for a comfortable, secure retirement.

Unfortunately, many workers retire today without the first two components in place for a secure retirement. The American saving rate inexorably declined to nearly zero, as banks and savings and loans cut interest rates so low that many people looked upon saving as a foolish or antiquated idea popular with their grandparents. New governmental programs designed to encourage saving (such as the 401 plans, Roth IRA, the standard IRA – even including a tax deductibility feature for lower paid employees – and savings bonds with annually adjusted interest rates) have not been able to substantially offset this trend. For many American workers, monthly credit card payments have replaced the weekly bank deposit.

More noticeable still is the disappearance of the traditional pension. In 1980, 83% of workers with pensions had "defined benefits" paid by their employers. Such programs usually guaranteed the retiree a regular monthly payment along with certain health insurance benefits (which sometimes also imposed a co-payment deducted from the retiree's pension). Today, the total enjoying such programs has shrunk to 21%, with many employees switched involuntarily from their "defined benefits" to self- directed (or "defined contributions") plans. By contrast with "defined benefits", the "defined contributions" programs promise the retiree a return of the tax-deferred income he deposited in one or more of a variety of plans the company offered (with the amounts he put in sometimes matched by his employer). These deposits usually increase in value over the years. Depending on the decisions made by the employee about his company's plans, he receives more or less at retirement, usually in a lump sum. Once the money is paid out, the company's obligation to the retiree ends.

Adding to the problem, many company managers cynically cancelled the workers' negotiated benefits altogether by filing for reorganization and contract cancellation through bankruptcy court proceedings. Although the Pension Benefit Guarantee Corporation (a federal agency) has assumed some of these obligations, the payments it provides are usually substantially lower than those negotiated through collective bargaining. Most upper level executives were able to do significantly better by including "Golden Parachutes" in their contracts, allowing them to retire with less severely impaired benefits.

Those who have thus come to depend upon Social Security payments to prevent poverty in their old age must not be deprived of the single remaining retirement security program they have. Promises have been made by the American people through their representatives and senators in Congress, and those promises must be honored.

Happily, many people are not totally dependent upon Social Security as their sole or primary source of retirement income. Those individuals who planned better or were more careful or lucky in preparing for "old age" and would remain relatively well off without Social Security's monthly payments can justly be required to forfeit a portion of their benefits.

The sum of $200,000 per year in income (excluding Social Security retirement benefits) would be designated as the dividing line between poverty and sufficient income. This figure represents an income of $4000 per week, an amount adequate to meet most people's real needs.

For each additional $1000 over $200,000, a Social Security recipient would forfeit 1% of his monthly retirement benefit. Thus, for example, if a person had an annual retirement income of $225,000 (or $25,000 above the threshold), his Social Security benefits would decrease by 25%. No retiree would lose his entire Social Security monthly payments until his income level reached $300,000 (a retirement income roughly equivalent to $25,000 per month). Of course, if the person's income subsequently decreased below the $200,000 threshold figure, his full Social Security retirement benefits would automatically be restored.

Such a moderate decrease in Social Security retirement payments relative to the person's income would not impose a severe hardship on any retiree nor force him into poverty. In addition to income, the person probably holds considerable property and other possessions, but these assets are not considered in the calculation of the

$200,000. The amount involves **only income** -- not net worth -- with Medicare and drug benefit coverage continuing.

Some might contend that it is unjust to "penalize" a person for saving regularly and planning wisely for his retirement years. While there certainly exists much merit in this objection, it fails to consider that the person may have already been "rewarded" during his pre-retirement life.

Any person who has accumulated enough wealth to ensure an annual income of at least $200,000 per year following his retirement has somehow made "the system" work for him. He might have inherited his wealth, been offered a well paid position based on family connections, made shrewd (or lucky) stock investments at just the right moment, studied for many years to prepare for a lucrative career, or met just the right person who provided prudent advice at some pivotal point in his life. Perhaps, as a top level executive for a major corporation, he was able to arrange a very lucrative "golden parachute" and a significant retirement pension.

Doubtlessly, many profited from governmental policies or programs. Inheritance taxes were maintained below a confiscatory level, while tax laws frequently provide advantages (or loopholes) useable only by wealthy individuals. Others were enabled to complete their education by receiving temporary (or sometimes permanent) exemption from selective service (the draft) or by securing tuition money through a government insured loan program. Some had families that lived in the right areas, whose neighbors financed (through government imposed taxation) well-equipped, outstanding schools. Of course, no one ought be criticized for using such programs to enhance his position, but "the system" that worked for him and now affords him a very comfortable retirement may justly impose a special obligation upon him.

On the other hand, everyone knows many people without a large retirement savings account who were unable to save for retirement because the low income they received for the work they performed had to be spent for immediate needs. Others were struck by a major catastrophe, such as a prolonged illness or caring for an aged relative, or faced the huge expense involved in raising and educating a child. Even those who denied themselves luxuries and vacations and worked faithfully, scrimping and saving, often were unable to build a large "nest egg" for their golden years. Indeed, Social Security was especially designed to enable conscientious workers such as these to retire with dignity and not beg for handouts or charity from those better off.

Obviously some ended up nearly penniless at retirement due to improvident spending or an extravagant lifestyle. They, along with the conscientious and less fortunate, will gain. Some may find in a means testing provision a justification for hand to mouth spending or maxing out their credit cards now, forcing others to care for them in the future. But, those who COULD save, but CHOSE not to, will be unable to continue to enjoy the extravagant lifestyle to which they have grown accustomed since their monthly retirement benefits are capped and will not be increased in any way if means testing is added to the Social Security program.

This feature, while seemingly unfair, best exemplifies the ideal of sharing the burden and benefits of Social

Security. Those who by family, chance, dedication, or wise use of existing programs made the "system" work to their benefit, now are enjoined by that very same "system" to insure the long-term welfare of those less capable, skillful, or lucky. Sharing the burdens and the benefits best applies when the benefits gained are substantial while the sacrifice entailed is minimal. With means testing, **Equity** can be insured for all retirees without truly impoverishing anyone.

In addition to equity, Social Security's long term **Sustainability** will be enhanced by the decreasing the amount of the program's retirement payments for those already having a substantial retirement income from other sources and not needing such additional income. This saved income can be used to create an even more **Comprehensive** system of new programs benefiting the elderly (such as providing eye glasses, laser treatment for glaucoma, or hearing aids) or to help offset the constantly rising cost of Medicare.

As with other parts of this program, **Predictability** is built in. An accurate estimate of the following year's additional income to Social Security can easily be made. All people who have any income must file a return with the Internal Revenue Service. Since one year's returns tend not to vary greatly from the previous year, a fairly accurate prediction of the taxpayer's anticipated income in a future year can be made. Similarly, an individual tax-payer can clearly determine whether or not his income has exceeded the threshold and by how much, which enables him to compute the adjustment of his payments from Social Security the following year.

This revision will be **Helpful to the Economy**, since the well off, continuing to enjoy a significant income even with their decreased Social Security retirement payments, will probably not crimp their expenditures, and the less well off will feel secure in spending with no threat to their monthly payment checks from a Social Security shortfall.

Optional Privately Controlled Savings Accounts

If the Plano Plan reforms were instituted, the resulting increased income and decreased expenditures would make proposals for instituting privately controlled savings accounts within the present Social Security program a realistic possibility.

Although a plethora of proposals have been offered, most of them contain very similar features. Almost all the proposals envision implementation of a plan replacing the present Social Security account of workers below a certain age with savings accounts controlled by the workers themselves. These new accounts would be financed by the Social Security taxes the worker paid (which would be credited to his savings account), but the investment decisions would be made by the worker himself. Gradually, as retired workers covered by the present Social Security system died, these new privately directed plans would replace the present payments system. Some plans require workers to choose among various mutual fund companies offering different investment options for their Social Security payments, while others would allow a greater latitude among financial investments considered relatively safe, such as Fortune 500 Company stock, A rated bonds, or FDIC insured CD's. The plans often envision certain limited, specific situations allowing workers pre-retirement withdrawals (for their own or their children's higher education, for the purchase of a first home, or to meet medical emergencies). At retirement, the worker would have immediate access to his savings (or some alternative pay-out plan providing set monthly payments), providing a greater or lesser amount depending upon the prudence of his investment. Medicare would be continued unchanged for all.

However, there is no reason why the federal government must **impose** such a plan upon all workers covered by Social Security (or on those below a certain age). Rather, the employees themselves could be allowed to select between two options: One would guarantee set retirement benefits for life (with a cap, the exact monthly payment, and annual benefit adjustments set by Congress), probably following some formula nearly identical to the one presently used (but with a cap on maximum payments for those paying very large amounts in taxes). The other option would set lower life-time monthly retirement payments (with the exact ratio set by Congress) for those choosing to invest their Social Security taxes in a less predictable, but potentially more lucrative, personal account.

This second option (of privately directed accounts), which would divert a portion of the worker's Social Security payments to investments in stocks, bonds, certificates of deposit, etc., might prove very attractive to young workers dubious about the long term sustainability of Social Security as funded today (or even as funded under the Plano Plan). The maximum amount the worker could divert under this plan would be limited, with approximately 1/2 of the worker's Social Security payments (or 3.0 % of the 6.2 % presently deducted from wages) most often suggested as a reasonable figure. Although some proponents favor building additional safeguards into the plan (such as requiring all investing be done through registered mutual funds), the protections already provided by the laws regulating the purchase, sale, and exchange of stocks and bonds seem sufficient to allow a person to use a private, licensed broker whom he trusts to help him select and purchase equities and bonds. His selections would be strictly limited to secure investments: mutual funds, the preference and common stock of long established companies (perhaps the Blue Chips, the Fortune 500, or the Standard and Poor's 100), very safe A - rated bonds, or the absolutely secure government insured CD's, Treasury Notes, or United States Savings Bonds.

For those choosing the personally directed account option, the remaining 1/2 of his tax (along with the matching 6.2% of his employer) would continue to guarantee him a basic retirement benefit of 3/4 the amount paid those selecting the standard benefit plan. If the person invested wisely, the personal savings account would increase his retirement benefits above those selecting the set benefits plan; if he chose unwisely, he would have less.

One major advantage of the privately controlled (or privately directed) account is that the worker would have immediate access to the privately invested funds as soon as he retired, allowing him to begin carrying out his retirement plans. In addition, the worker would (under most plans) also be allowed the opportunity to use part of his private account funds prior to his retirement for legitimate purposes which would increase his income or security in the future, such as making the down payment on his first house, paying the expenses for his own or his children's education, or meeting sudden medical expenses. Since many of these high ticket expenses are already partially addressed by Federal Government programs (Veteran's Administration Insured Home Loans, G.I. Bill Education and Pell grants, 529 College Savings Plans, and the frequently discussed Medical Savings Plan), adjusting Social Security to augment or complement them should not prove that difficult.

As with other parts of the Plano Plan, the accounts must be phased in gradually (a caution put forth by former Federal Reserve Chairman Allen Greenspan). For the first year or even longer, individual account eligibility could be limited to those over 60 years of age, likely resulting in few enrollees because the program offers few advantages for those so close to retirement. The following year (or even after two or three years to test the systems being used), the age of eligibility could be lowered to 55, which might possibly draw a somewhat larger number, especially among those whose higher incomes were now becoming fully subject to the 6.2 % rate but whose monthly retirement payments are capped. The ages would be lowered still more in succeeding years, as experience showed its practical workability and financial experts could gauge more accurately its long-range impact on investment and the national economy in general. Eventually all workers would be asked to irrevocably select between the alternatives by a certain age (most likely at around 25 or 30), just as today's retirees must choose irrevocably from alternative retirement ages with their respective benefits and drawbacks.

We ought not conclude the workers of the United States are so incompetent that they could not manage their own retirement savings plans successfully. More and more companies require their employees to assume greater responsibility for their retirement planning by switching from a company controlled defined benefit plans to self-directed accounts (such as 401k or similar plans, with new employees automatically enrolled and with contributions often matched by their employers). Already the federal and state governments insist adults control financial affairs on their own during their adult years with governmental supervision only to prevent fraud. Must we assume a person lacks similar abilities if given **limited** control of an account involving 3% of his income ?

When people face new situations (such as using a computer at the worksite, operating cell phones or entirely novel kinds of cameras, choosing from among a myriad of options for phone service and energy providers, or self check-out of their grocery purchases), they quickly learn the skills needed to handle those new tasks. Ask any college student (or anyone who has moved from his parents' home) how he learned to do his own laundry, make edible and varied meals, and live within a budget. When he has to do these tasks for himself, he picks up the skills needed (and gains greater personal independence as a bonus). It is probable the same thing will occur when the person assumes the greater risk (and the potentially greater gain) of controlling a personal retirement account. On the other hand, if the person doubts his own financial ability, feels unsure about making correct financial decisions, or prefers having someone else supervise (and guarantee) his retirement funding, he may decline the personal account, remaining with the present assured payments plan.

Adding personal savings plans insures greater **Sustainability** for Social Security in the long term. Fears that a Social Security system containing privately directed savings accounts would be unable to provide promised benefits are groundless if other parts of the Plano Plan are instituted. The diversion to privately controlled savings accounts are more than offset by increasing revenue (if the cap on earnings is removed) and by decreasing expenditures (as a limit on benefits is set, the age of retirement rises, and means testing begins). Even if all of the Plano Plan was rejected (except the indispensable gradual removal of the cap on wages taxed) and almost all workers switched to individually directed personal savings accounts (which could only occur over a number of years), the amount of funds coming into Social Security to provide pensions for those under the current system would not decrease greatly, if at all, because the removal of the cap on wages taxed as well as the probable annual increase in wages for all workers would provide sufficient funds. In addition, the decrease in income to Social Security would not exceed 1/2 of the employees' wages (with funding still maintained from the full 6.2% tax paid by employers). After 15 or 20 years (or perhaps even less), the amount of money required for Social Security pensions will begin to decrease annually as more individuals with privately controlled savings accounts reach retirement age (and receive 3/4 payments).

Indeed, a person might argue that privately directed savings accounts are required to maintain **Equity,** if the cap on wages taxed is removed. Since a very well paid worker would be required to pay a greater amount of money in Social Security taxes (though the same percentage as every other employee) and his monthly payment after retirement are capped, he will probably pay in more than he will receive back. Although there is no injustice in this (since all taxpayers are required to share the burden of government services based on an ability to pay and receive a reasonable share of the benefits in return), fairness suggests that anyone who pays a larger amount should be allowed to invest at least a part of his larger Social Security tax payment in a way he thinks most beneficial to himself, while an equal amount is used to support the retirement of other less well paid workers. No one loses or gains a financial advantage by the selection of one plan over another since those already retired continue to receive their promised Social Security payments and those still working are required to pay the same rate and amount regardless of the alternative chosen.

In addition to providing potential benefits to the holders, these personal accounts would prove very **Helpful to the Economy**. When the United States government needs to borrow money to fund programs and cannot sell all its Treasury notes and bonds to American investors, it must secure the necessary funding from foreign sources. Competing against other nations' and private corporations' financial instruments, it must offer investors higher interest rates (fueling domestic inflation) and give non-Americans greater influence over our economy by the threat of refusing to buy, by demanding higher interest, or even by suddenly selling off the notes they already hold. Like the federal government, private corporations constantly require new revenue to finance ventures and support promising but expensive research and development. When that money must be obtained from overseas, foreign investors often insist that some of the investment be used to benefit their nation's workers and economy.

By contrast, the availability of such funding from personal accounts (and mutual funds) practically guarantees eager buyers for the absolutely secure federal bonds and Treasury short term T-bills (which might be the only financial instruments handled by some mutual funds and be purchased by other funds as a secure hedge against stock and bond market adjustments). The funds would also spur investment in American industries and discourage the exporting of jobs to foreign countries since the company must maintain American employment to insure the availability of present and future financing from personal accounts (not to mention the wrath of share voting workers who invested their retirement savings in the company).

Absolute **Predictability** is not possible with this part of the program, since that depends on the number of workers choosing privately directed savings accounts (instead of staying with the present plan) and the speed at which the plan is fully implemented. However, the numbers would most likely be increasing slowly, allowing fairly accurate predictions as the program develops.

The **Comprehensiveness** of Social Security programs would not be harmed by the gradual conversion from an all government program to a public/private blending.

Sufficient funds would remain available to fund present programs (including present retirement payments and Medicare and the prescription drug benefit) as private plans were phased in. Thus the introduction of privately directed accounts will have no effect on the payments currently made to retirees nor on the benefits paid to those soon to retire.

THE NEED FOR PROMPT AND PRUDENT ACTION

The need for prompt Congressional action to reformulate Social Security is by now obvious to everyone. The problems confronting the system cannot be wished away, nor will they simply disappear if we ignore them long enough. Inaction by Congress now will only make the problems worse, until eventually the situation will be labeled a "CRISIS" and result in a hasty, possibly ill-conceived, temporary patch-up job rather than the comprehensive reformulation required.

Until now, three alternative plans have been presented: A drastic rise in Social Security taxes (presumably maintaining the present cap on wages), or redeeming the totally valueless, fictitious Social Security Trust Fund Bonds, or reducing retirement benefits (either gradually or as soon as the "Bonds" are paid off).

As I have shown, none of these proposed solutions (nor any combination of them) could possibly solve the Social Security funding problem. Furthermore, each of these "solutions" would impose a severe burden upon one or more groups in our population, pitting one pressure group against another as each vainly attempted to preserve for its members some particular, cherished advantage. Instead of displaying common sense and a willingness to share the burden and benefits by devising a plan to meet the needs of all generations, each group would virtually shout (like a spoiled child) "ME FIRST! ME FIRST! I DON'T CARE IF THE OTHERS GET NOTHING!"

Common sense, as well as the system's long-term sustainability and equity, demands a better solution. America's elected representatives in Congress need to quickly fashion a truly comprehensive program to address the needs of the nation's aging population. The 2000 census shows the median age (with ½ of the population above and ½ of the population below that age) has climbed to an all-time high of 35.3 years, compared to 32.9 in 1990 and 30 in 1980. More frightening still was that the most rapid increase (at 49%) was shown in the age group 45-54. The oldest of this group (now 51-60) can begin applying for retirement benefits in 2008. Waiting until later to address the problem will be waiting too long.

Raising the Social Security taxes for all workers at or below the present slowly rising cap or taking the money from general taxation simply will not work. When the retired population spirals upward after 2008, the new expense will dwarf the present annual $ 574 Billion cost of retirement benefits. If the cap on earnings taxed is not removed, the present Social Security tax would have to at least double from its present 6.2 % (plus 1.45 % for Medicare) to 14 %, with some estimating the needed increase as high as 20 %, which combined with other taxes would be a confiscatory rate on the least well-paid workers. Raising the general revenue rates for all tax-payers is equally ineffective since the Entitlement Programs (including Social Security) consume over ½ of the federal spending already, and experts assume the amount will only grow over the years, while the amounts needed for homeland security, maintaining the military, building roads, educating the children, etc. will not be declining. The diversion of such a large amount from other needs to Social Security retirement payments would quickly cripple the economy and harm the nation's future welfare.

The second alternative (redeeming the Social Security Trust Fund Bonds) is pure fantasy! As pointed out several times above, the money to pay off the bonds simply doesn't exist anywhere. Pretending, day dreaming, or wishing it wasn't so will not make the money suddenly rematerialize. The money collected (like all taxes) was Congress's to spend as it thought best, and past Congresses spent every penny. Their I.O.U.'s (the Social Security Trust Fund Bonds) remain, but they have absolutely no value (being nothing more than a receipt for money spent) with future Congresses free to cancel them at will. If Congress chooses to continue payments (and it probably will) and with no additional reform, it will have to draw the money from present tax revenues, which will require either higher taxes or more borrowing (beyond the $ 9 Trillion limit already authorized).

The final alternative (cutting benefits) would represent the cruelest choice for the millions (58% of the retired population according to the AARP) who look upon Social Security's monthly payments as a major source of income. With more and more companies lowering the amount of pensions and benefits given, converting defined benefit programs to self-directed retirement plans, or ruthlessly cutting pensions entirely, the Social

Security check is increasingly the differerence between a satisfactory retirement and poverty. Few have sufficient savings to offset the loss of buying power resulting from the loss of the monthly government check. Congress (as spokesperson for all Americans) has repeatedly pledged to care for the elderly and retired. Those promises to retirees (along with the promises made to workers now paying their taxes regularly who are planning their futures based upon those pledges) must continue to be honored. Present retirees have sustained the Social Security system by their taxes for over 70 years and rightly expect to receive their promised reward.

Instead of the two draconian measures or the lunacy of somehow planning to make payments using worthless bonds, the Plano Plan offers practical solutions. Eliminating the cap on wages taxed steadily but gradually will increase the system's income, while adjusting the monthly retirement payments (with no one, except those subject to means testing, getting less than they presently receive), slowly raising the age of retirement, and instituting means testing will decrease its expenses. Combining these steps will guarantee the **Sustainability and Equity** of Social Security. Introducing privately controlled accounts into the Social Security system adds an additional level of equity without endangering the system's overall sustainability.

Adopting all the changes suggested in the Plano Plan fairly apportions the burdens and benefits of Social Security among all: Working people, businesses, and retirees.

Workers earning higher wages will be subject to new taxes on the part of their incomes above $100,000, but their "new" rate makes it exactly equal to that paid all along by their less well compensated colleagues. The increased revenue from the gradual removal of the cap on wages taxed will probably be relatively small at first despite the annual increases. Although more of a person's income would be subject to tax because of the higher cap, the number of workers earning those higher wages is smaller. For example, there are significantly fewer workers earning $500,000 than those being paid $125,000. Taxation on huge incomes (say, over a million dollars) does not occur until the 14th or 15th year of the plan.

Younger worker will have to plan on working longer before being eligible for retirement, but the slow rise in the retirement age of three months per year allows gradual adaptation and is more than offset by the greater surety that they will eventually receive their entire monthly benefits.

Businesses will have plenty of time to adjust to higher labor cost as the cap slowly rises. The gradual nature of the increases allows corporations to anticipate and adjust to the changing situation among their better paid employees (and perhaps requiring their Boards of Directors to make some corrections in the compensations paid to senior executives).

Very few retirees (since it affects only those having retirement incomes over $200,000 per year) will find decreases in their monthly payments, and all will still continue to receive cost of living increases at least equal to the rate of inflation (with a annual cap at 8 % for those above 150% of the poverty level and 12 % for those below that figure). The few retirees subject to means testing (those receiving more than $200,000 annually from non-

Social Security sources) will realize the loss of part or all of their Social Security payments will only minimally affect their standard of living.

The expenses of Social Security, at first declining due to the delay in the age of eligibility for retirement payments, the two-tiered adjustment of monthly payments, and the introduction of means testing, will increase as more reach the later age for retirement (and receive payments) and automatic annual adjustments increase the amounts paid. On the other hand, adding privately directed savings accounts will at first decrease income, but 10 to 20 years later will increase the money available in the Social Security fund. In the intervening period, the income (from the general increase in wages and the taxation of higher incomes) should more than offset the increase in expenses. Once fully implemented, the reformulation will result in a steady, annual surplus.

Social Security's increased revenue (once the plan is fully implemented) will allow not only the maintenance of present programs but also an expansion of Social Security benefits creating a more **Comprehensive** system to meet the needs of the increasingly greater number of older, retired Americans.

Since all of these proposed changes would be implemented according to a predetermined schedule, the changes are fully **Predictable** and, as I tried to show for each suggestion given above, none would be significantly **Harmful to the Economy.**

However, Congress must do two additional things to bring about a true reformulation of Social Security.

First, it must promise (as far as it can bind future Congresses) that it will not modify, change, adjust, or fiddle with Social Security for 20 years. Unless the system shows itself in immediate danger of total disintegration (a true and severe crisis), Congress must agree to leave the reformulated Social Security system unchanged (like a plane on auto-pilot whose crew need do nothing unless an unexpected squall suddenly forms). Congress likes few things better than to "improve" a well running system, which, though sometimes helpful, frequently is done without sufficient foresight to anticipate the undesirable consequences of even minor reforms. The Plano Plan stresses total **Predictability** which allows businesses, workers, and retirees to plan their lives with a high degree of certainty about their financial situation in the years ahead. As James Madison said, "It will be of little avail to the people that the laws are made by men of their own choice if the laws ... be repealed or revised before they are promulgated, or undergo such incessant changes that no man, who knows what the law is today, can guess what it will be like tomorrow."

As soon as this plan is approved, clever individuals will undoubtedly see flaws and suggest "necessary" reforms or alterations to improve the lives of retirees or workers. All such reform proposals should immediately be stuffed into a folder labeled "For Consideration in 2027". No system devised by the human mind is flawless (alas, including the Plano Plan), and no program near perfect now will be so 20 years in the future, but most parts of the Plano Plan are deliberately designed to be implemented slowly and deliberately, with one part frequently offsetting the potentially harmful effects of another. For example, the phased introduction of privately directed savings plans is sensible only when combined with the gradual removal of the cap on earnings taxed. The privately directed accounts will drain money from the program, which will be offset by the extra tax income received from the removal of the cap on wages, maintaining stability within the system. In 20 years, with the plan fully implemented, the flaws made visible can be removed. By then all the suggested changes will have undergone a thorough and thoughtful evaluation without the urgency felt when the whole system is in imminent danger of collapse (a "crisis").

The second thing Congress must do is to mandate that any surplus which results from the Plano Plan (which is likely once most of the Plan has been implemented) will be used solely as a set aside prepaying the following year's anticipated benefits, for Social Security related expenses (i.e., Medicare, the Prescription Drug Benefit, other improvements introduced, and if necessary, salvaging the Pension Benefit Guarantee Corporation), or to help pay down the huge national debt. The 1983 Bipartisan Social Security Rescue Plan, designed to create a savings account for later anticipated expenses, soon turned into a handy piggy-bank for immediate expenses, with the Social Security Trust Fund Bonds nothing more than paper I.O.U.'s stuffed into the emptied bank. This must not be repeated. Any surplus income over expenses must be strictly dedicated to benefiting retirees and improving the comprehensiveness of Social Security services or to paying down the National Debt, an action which benefits not only retirees but also everyone whose sees his investments and savings eroded by the nation's increased indebtedness. (I'm assuming Congress would not act so blatantly felonious as to create a program and pay for it by expanding the National Debt by an amount equal to Social Security's anticipated extra income from that year.)

Everyone realizes that federal budget deficits year after year are creating an enormous and ultimately unsustainable debt. Future federal budgets must not only pay for all the expenses for the following year, they must begin to pay down the national debt. Such balanced budgets are impossible unless the expenses of Social Security (which will balloon as the Baby Boomers begin collecting their benefits in 2008) are addressed first. The Plano Plan is designed to handle just that problem.